WHILE I WAIT

Jennifer Fancher

ISBN 978-1-0980-4348-3 (paperback)
ISBN 978-1-0980-4349-0 (digital)

Christian Faith Publishing, Inc.
832 Park Avenue
Meadville, PA 16335
www.christianfaithpublishing.com

Printed in the United States of America

I would like to dedicate this book to my wonderful Daddy. You are my best friend and hero! I have never known a moment that I did not have your complete love and support. That bond has shaped me into the woman I am today. Thank you for waiting for me and for teaching me how to wait. I love you so much!

I would also like to thank my wonderful family and amazing friends! You have loved me, supported me, encouraged me, and guided me. I am forever grateful that the Lord has blessed me with each and every one of you!

Chapter 1

Wait
The Most Difficult Answer

I like to deal in the definitive. "Yes" and "No" are the rulers of my comfort zone. While hearing either of these answers can at times be unpleasant, at least I know where I stand. This gives me freedom to adjust to the situation within the ease of my comfort zone. I am perfectly happy in this state; nothing is uncertain and everything is spelled out. Unfortunately, life has brought a different answer to my door, "Wait."

What am I supposed to do with "Wait"? The entire concept shatters my comfort zone. After a few years of asking this question incredulously, I began to ask it in earnest. While at first "Wait" was annoying, it quickly became one of the most difficult answers to hear. As my prayers became deeper and my desires became more pressing, my desperation for a "Yes" or "No" became overwhelming. I found myself genuinely struggling. A question began to emerge in my heart: Could my faith withstand the test of having to wait?

Everyone is waiting for something. We all have a prayer we are lifting up with earnest to God who has yet to provide an answer. There are probably many other things He has given—strength, wisdom, support, love, courage—but not a definitive answer. In this fact, I find a strange sense of comfort. I am not alone. You are not alone. This is a battle we all have to endure. Many times during my own battle, I have been brought back to the Word of God.

It has given me comfort in the midst of overwhelming pain. What He has brought to my attention is the fact that many of the most amazing examples of faith had to wait.

One of the things I love the most about the Word of God is the honesty. God doesn't just show us the successes of the men and women whose lives He shares with us, He also gives us details of their failures. Because of this, while I read through the list of people who had to wait, I get to see their raw responses. I have failed so often with this test, it is encouraging to know that I am not alone in that. However, the most important thing for me to know and learn is how they overcame their failure.

Take a trip through the Word with me and allow me to share with you my precious group of encouragers:

Sarah: Sarah was the wife of Abraham. Abraham was not only amazingly wealthy, he was also a friend of God. God spoke directly to him on multiple occasions. Sarah had everything going for her. She was very beautiful, her husband was well off, and they had a good relationship with God. There was just one thing missing, which turned out to be a huge thing.

We learn in Genesis 11:30 that Sarah was barren; she had no children. In that time period, one's value as a woman was based solely on her ability to bear a male heir. While Sarah had everything else, she did not have what others would consider most important. Finally, in Genesis 12:2, Abraham is promised an heir by God. This promise is reaffirmed in Genesis 15:1–5. Imagine the excitement that they must have felt! Except that promise came with a contingency, they had to wait for God's timing. As the years passed and Sarah's time gap for being physically able to bear children closed, Sarah became tired of waiting for God. She tried to force His hand in Genesis 16 with horrible consequences. She eventually just gave up. In Genesis 18:11, we find her having passed the age of childbearing.

I want to pause here and bring to mind the pain and disappointment she must have felt. She was promised this and yet, she had endured month after month, year after year of empty arms, until human reasoning would say all hope was gone. God's response to her pain is found in Genesis 18:14. God planned to go outside the confines of the natural laws of reproduction and demonstrate His power. His plan and timing was different than Sarah's. While she had to endure years of unbearable pain, we find in Genesis 21 that she finally received God's promise.

Rebekah: Rebekah was the wife of Isaac, the son of promise. We find in Genesis 25:21 that Rebekah was also barren. If you compare Genesis 25:20 with Genesis 25:26, we learn that Isaac prayed for her to conceive for twenty years. In God's timing, their prayer was answered, and Rebekah became pregnant with Jacob and Esau.

Rachel: Rachel was the wife of Jacob. Theirs was a marriage of love, and Jacob also became very wealthy. Unfortunately, Rachel was barren. Jacob was also married to her sister Leah, who had son after son after son. This doubled Rachel's pain, and we find her reaching her breaking point in Genesis 30:1. She would rather be dead than endure the pain and humiliation any longer. What a raw response! Have you ever felt that way? Where you scream out in pain that if God makes you wait one more day for your prayer to be answered, you would rather be dead? We learn that her frustration with God's timing does not stop her prayers, and in Genesis 30:22–23, we see that God listens to her and grants her a child.

Joseph: Joseph was the son of Jacob and Rachel. His life went from one of ease to one of hardship very quickly. After being betrayed by the ones who should have loved and protected him, he was sold into slavery. Then, after doing the right thing and saying "No" to sin, he was imprisoned. During his time in prison, he interprets two dreams and asked to be remembered by the butler. In Genesis 41:1, we find that he had to wait in an Egyptian prison for two years before he was remembered and restored.

There is something special to me about the story of Joseph. We are allowed to see the perfection in the timing of God. Joseph had to be sold into slavery to get to Potiphar's house in Egypt. Joseph had to be sent to prison to meet the butler. Joseph had to wait in prison for the butler to introduce him at the right time to Pharaoh. Because he endured and waited, he became second in Egypt and was able to save the entire nation and his whole family.

Hannah: Hannah was the wife of Elkanah and the mother of Samuel. We learn in 1 Samuel 1:2 that Hannah had to wait for Samuel. Unfortunately, it was not a comfortable, painless period of waiting. 1 Samuel 1:6 tells us that Elkanah's other wife made Hannah's life as miserable as possible. When she brought her pain to God, she was praying privately, but so fervently Eli thought that she was drunk. God hears the pain and desperation of her heart and blesses her with a son. After she dedicates him to God, God blesses her with five more children. Her prayer of thanksgiving in 1 Samuel 2:1–10 shows a heart that endured pain but never gave up on God.

David: David was the second king of Israel and a man after God's own heart. David went from being like a son to King Saul, the best friend of the prince Jonathan, and the husband of the princess Michal, to a man who was daily running for his life. Even though God had already promised him the kingdom, the years following that promise were ones of difficulty and despair. David wrote a great deal of the Psalms, and we can see his deep struggle with the pain of waiting for restoration and relief. Psalm 27:14, Psalm 33:20–22, Psalm 40:1–3, Psalm 62:5–8, and Psalm 69 show a heart that is bleeding but still clinging to God in the midst of trial.

Elizabeth: Elizabeth was the mother of John the Baptist. She, like Sarah, had a child in her old age. We find in Luke 1:24–25 her response, "The Lord has taken away my reproach among the people"; such a simple statement that displays so much grief. After enduring years of ridicule and rejection, God shows mercy and grants her petition.

Paul: Paul was an apostle of Christ. He was a great man who was mighty in faith; he was also sick. We find in 2 Corinthians 12:7–8 that he prayed multiple times to be healed. He also had a great desire to work with many different congregations and had to wait before he was able to finally see them again (Romans 1:13).

The Unnamed Woman: The woman in Luke 8:43–48 had a "flow of blood" that she had suffered with for twelve years. She had done everything she could think of to be cured; nothing worked. Her final act of desperation was to reach for the border of the garment of the Great Healer. Through her display of faith and trust in the Lord, God answered her prayer and brought health to her broken body.

Jesus: My merciful Friend and Savior left the glory and splendor of heaven to come to earth, live a poor and distressing life, and die a horrible and painful death for my sins. He had to wait for thirty-three years to be reunited with His Father in His rightful place. He continues to wait patiently for untold millions to accept Him or to return to Him. He waits for the day when all of us will be with Him in heaven. He waits for me to trust Him and His timing.

To draw to a close, I simply wish to state, if you are being asked to wait, you are in good company. While some of these examples received a "Yes" to their prayers, others did not. Despite the answer they received in the end, I want to focus on the strength they gained through waiting. Throughout the rest of this study, we will look at different aspects of how to wait. I invite you to close your eyes, take hold of God's hand, and join me in weathering the storm of waiting.

Chapter 2

Waiting in Faith

"Now faith is the reality of what is hoped
for, the proof of what is not seen." Hebrews 11:1

I would like to start this journey by asking you to genuinely
look into your heart. The following is a list of verses that come from
the depths of God's heart, a plea for you to have faith in Him and
to trust Him. As you read through these verses, I ask that you stop
and meditate on each section. Take a few minutes to write down how
these words from God affect your heart and/or what you learned
from them. At the end of this section, my questions for you to pon-
der are these: Do you have faith in Him? What will your response be?

"There is a way that seems right to a man,
but its end is the way to death." Proverbs 14:12

"To humans belong the plans of the heart,
but from the Lord comes the proper answer of the
tongue. All a person's ways seem pure to them,
but motives are weighed by the Lord. Commit to
the Lord whatever you do, and He will establish
your plans. The Lord works out everything to its
proper end—even the wicked for a day of disas-
ter." Proverbs 16:1–4

"The mind of a man plans his way, but the Lord directs his steps." Proverbs 16:9

My thoughts on these verses:

_____

_____

_____

_____

"Hope deferred makes the heart sick, but when the desire comes, it is a tree of life." Proverbs 13:12

"The Lord is near to the broken-hearted and saves the crushed in spirit." Psalm 34:18

"For His anger lasts only a moment, but His favor, a lifetime. Weeping may endure for a night, but joy comes in the morning." Psalm 30:5

"Do not fear, for I am with you; do not be afraid, for I am your God. I will strengthen you; I will help you; I will hold on to you with My righteous right hand." Isaiah 41:10

"And let us not grow weary of doing good, for in due season we will reap, if we do not give up." Galatians 6:9

"Be anxious for nothing, but in everything by prayer and supplication with thanksgiving let your requests be made known to God. And the peace of God, which surpasses all comprehension, will guard your hearts and your minds in Christ Jesus." Philippians 4:6–7

"Therefore I tell you, do not worry about your life, what you will eat or drink; or about your body, what you will wear. Is not life more than food, and the body more than clothes? Look at the birds of the air; they do not sow or reap or store away in barns, and yet your heavenly Father feeds them. Are you not much more valuable than they? Can any one of you by worrying add a single hour to your life? And why do you worry about clothes? See how the flowers of the field grow. They do not labor or spin. Yet I tell you that not even Solomon in all his splendor was dressed like one of these. If that is how God clothes the grass of the field, which is here today and tomorrow is thrown into the fire, will he not much more clothe you—you of little faith? So do not worry, saying, 'What shall we eat?' or 'What shall we drink?' or 'What shall we wear?' For the pagans run after all these things, and your heavenly Father knows that you need them. But seek first His kingdom and His righteousness, and all these things will be given to you as well. Therefore do not worry about tomorrow, for tomorrow will worry about itself. Each day has enough trouble of its own." Matthew 6:25–34

My thoughts on these verses:

_____

_____

_____

_____

"This God, His way is perfect; the word of the Lord proves true; He is a shield for all who take refuge in Him." Psalm 18:30

"My thoughts are nothing like your thoughts,' says the Lord. 'And my ways are far beyond anything you could imagine. For just as the heavens are higher than the earth, so My ways are higher than your ways and My thoughts higher than your thoughts.'" Isaiah 55:8–9

"God is greater than our heart, and He knows everything." 1 John 3:20

"But do not forget this one thing, dear friends: With the Lord, a day is like a thousand years, and a thousand years are like a day. The Lord is not slow in keeping His promises, as some understand slowness. Instead, He is patient with you, not wanting anyone to perish, but everyone to come to repentance." 2 Peter 3:8–9

"Declaring the end from the beginning and from ancient times things not yet done, saying, 'My counsel shall stand, and I will accomplish all My purpose.'" Isaiah 46:10

My thoughts on these verses:

_____

_____

_____

_____

"For I know the plans I have for you," declares the Lord, "plans to prosper you and not to harm you, plans to give you hope and a future. Then you will call on Me and come and pray to Me, and I will listen to you." Jeremiah 29:11–12

"At the right time, I, the Lord, will make it happen" Isaiah 60:22

"There is a time for everything, and a season for every activity under the heavens" Ecclesiastes 3:1

"He has made everything beautiful in its time. He has also set eternity in the human heart; yet no one can fathom what God has done from beginning to end." Ecclesiastes 3:11

My thoughts on these verses:

_____

_____

_____

_____

"I have loved you with an everlasting love; therefore, I have continued to extend faithful love to you." Jeremiah 31:3

"Yet this I call to mind and therefore I have hope: Because of the Lord's great love we are not consumed, for His compassions never fail. They are new every morning; great is Your faithfulness. 'The Lord is my portion', says my soul, 'therefore I will hope in Him'. The Lord is good to those whose hope is in Him, to the one who seeks Him; it is good to wait quietly for the salvation of the Lord." Lamentations 3:21–26

"The Lord is good, a stronghold in a day of distress; He cares for those who take refuge in Him." Nahum 1:7

My thoughts on these verses:

_____

_____

_____

_____

"In the day of my trouble I call upon You, for You answer me." Psalm 86:7

"Submit yourselves therefore to God. Resist the devil, and he will flee from you. Draw near to God, and He will draw near to you." James 4:7–8

"Humble yourselves, therefore, under the mighty hand of God so that at the proper time He may exalt you, casting all your anxieties on Him, because He cares for you." 1 Peter 5:6–7

"Now to Him who is able to do far more abundantly than all that we ask or think, according to the power at work within us, to Him be glory in the church and in Christ Jesus throughout all generations, forever and ever. Amen." Ephesians 3:20–21

My thoughts on these verses:

_____

_____

_____

_____

"Trust in the Lord with all your heart and lean not on your own understanding; in all your ways submit to Him, and He will make your paths straight." Proverbs 3:5–6

"Now without faith it is impossible to please God, for the one who draws near to Him must believe that He exists and rewards those who seek Him." Hebrews 11:6

"By faith Sarah, herself, received power to conceive, even when she was past the age, since she considered Him faithful who had promised." Hebrews 11:11

"And we know that in all things God works for the good of those who love Him, who have been called according to His purpose." Romans 8:28

My thoughts on these verses:

_____

_____

_____

_____

"But they who wait for the Lord shall renew their strength; they shall mount up with wings like eagles; they shall run and not be weary; they shall walk and not faint." Isaiah 40:31

"From of old no one has heard or perceived by the ear, no eye has seen a God besides you, who acts for those who wait for Him." Isaiah 64:4

"Wait for the Lord; be strong, and let your heart take courage; wait for the Lord!" Psalm 27:14

"Delight yourself in the Lord, and He will give you the desires of your heart." Psalm 37:4

My thoughts on these verses:

_____

_____

_____

_____

While undergoing the trial of waiting, it is very easy to listen to the lies of Satan and believe that God does not hear you, want you, or love you. It may even get so bad that you wonder if He is even there or if He has the power to answer your prayer. I put so many verses in this chapter because I want you to experience the same sense of overwhelming truth that I experienced. God is there and is able. God hears me. God wants me. God loves me. God knows what He is doing.

If you are like me, you have spent many tear-filled nights asking or crying out the question of "Why?" "Why won't you answer me?" "Why are you withholding the thing I want the most?" "Why, of all people, are you asking me to wait?" This list of verses gave me my answer: God is working. I don't know how, I don't know why, and I have no clue as to the timeline. But God is working.

Someone once told me that God wants us to wait so that we know that the best blessings in life come only from Him. This idea is confirmed in James 1:17. It is a humbling truth that we often want to take credit for the blessings He allows us to possess. When we are asked to wait, it takes our eyes off ourselves and puts them back on God. We must trust Him and His timing.

None of this is easy. Your faith is in the midst of a difficult test. Unfortunately, I cannot give you a recipe to get rid of your pain. But if you believe Him, your faith will produce a balm that will ease the charred remains of your heart. It will give you peace and comfort when nothing else works. It will help you to seek God instead of sinful vices to ease the hurt. It will give you the only thing that will actually help get you through the trial: hope.

I encourage you to read through the verses again. Let them flow over your soul in a soothing tide. Now, pray. Cast your cares on Him. Tell Him what your heart desires and how hard it is to wait. Let Him know you trust Him and His timing. Ask Him for strength and peace to endure the trial. Take your eyes off the clock and put them on the One who loves you most and knows what you need before you ask Him. Allow Him to guide your life with wisdom; Understand that what you may be asking for might not be the best thing for you and, like a loving Father, He must protect His child. Know that there are moving pieces you simply cannot see. He can and is working everything for your good. He wants you to spend eternity with Him more than anything. That's why He willingly sent His Son to die for you. Let Him pave the pathway that will lead you to heaven. While it is hard right now, there is nothing in this universe more worthwhile.

In closing, I would like you to reflect one more time on the questions I brought to your mind at the beginning: Do you have faith in Him? What will your response be?

May He grant us faith to trust in His timing.

"And remember, I am with you always, to the end of the age." Matthew 28:20

Chapter 3

Waiting in Trust

In the previous chapter, we covered a couple of the vital verses on trusting God.

> "Trust in the Lord with all your heart and lean not on your own understanding; in all your ways submit to Him, and He will make your paths straight." Proverbs 3:5–6

> "Be anxious for nothing, but in everything by prayer and supplication with thanksgiving let your requests be made known to God. And the peace of God, which surpasses all comprehension, will guard your hearts and your minds in Christ Jesus." Philippians 4:6–7

I would like to delve into both of these a little deeper. Now that we have established the fact that God knows what He is doing and the importance of believing it, let's take the next step: Trust. Part of the difficulty of waiting is the anxiety of what the final answer will be. Questions begin to emerge such as, "What if there is truly no one for me to marry?" "What if I am unable to become a parent?" "What if I or my loved one never recover?" "What if my loved one never comes back to God?" "What if I am unable to get a job?" These doubts plague our hearts until we are frozen with anxiety.

That is where trust comes in. We must have the attitude, "No matter what happens, God is with me and He will give me the strength to endure it." This is so much easier said than done. So how do we get there? One step at a time. Let's take that step together.

It begins with perspective. You must take a step back and try to see the big picture. We can read about many people who prayed fervently to God for the desires of their heart. Some got a "Yes," however, many did not. With all of them there was a reason for their answer.

I would also ask that you consider that you don't actually know why you are asked to endure this trial. We have three examples in Scripture to explain why things happen: God is testing, Satan is tempting, and time/chance.

> "Consider a great joy, my brothers, whenever you experience various trials, knowing that the testing of your faith produces endurance. But endurance must do its complete work, so that you may be mature and complete, lacking nothing." James 1:2–4

> "Satan answered the Lord, 'Does Job fear God for nothing? Haven't You placed a hedge around him, his household, and everything he owns? You have blessed the work of his hands, and his possessions have increased in the land. But stretch out Your hand and strike everything he owns, and he will surely curse You to Your face." "Skin for skin!' Satan answered the Lord. 'A man will give up everything he owns in exchange for his life. But stretch out Your hand and strike his flesh and bones, and he will surely curse You to Your face." Job 1:9–11, 2:4–5

> "Again, I saw under the sun that the race is not to the swift, or the battle to the strong, or

bread to the wise, or riches to the discerning, or favor to the skillful; rather time and chance happen to all of them." Ecclesiastes 9:11

Regardless of the reason, your decision to trust in God for strength and guidance must be steadfast. I would encourage you not to get caught up in asking why this is happening to you. From experience, it is a dark and dangerous road that does not provide any helpful resolutions. This is where trust becomes your lifeline. I don't know what is going to happen or why this is happening, but I know that God has got me. I know that if I can make it through this, I will be one step closer to heaven.

So when we pray to Him we must believe, without a shadow of a doubt, that He will provide. What He will provide may not be what you are asking for, however, it will always be what you need. Instead of getting what you are asking for, He may give you the strength to endure, family/friends to lift you up and support you, forgiveness for weak moments, ease in other areas of life so that you can endure, peace in the storm, or hope for the future. The answer may be wait, but He will never ask you to do it without help. Let your heart trust in that.

The first step to trust is to look at the prayers that He has already answered. When our hearts have to do without something they are longing for, it is easy to make that the focus of every moment. So let's break that focus and reflect, not on what we do not have, but what we do have. I will start the list, and I encourage you to continue it.

A God who loves us
His Word and Holy Spirit that guides us
His Son who died for us
A beautiful world to live in
Family and friends to surround us with love and
happiness
A church family to encourage us and help us
Food to eat
Clothing on our backs and shoes on our feet

Shelter to live in
Electricity
Health care
Clean water
Indoor plumbing
Air conditioning
Heating
Transportation
Technology
Jobs
Education
The ability to enjoy experiences
Freedom
Safety
A multitude of physical blessings (who here has ever had a garage sale?)
Many prayers already answered (list at least three)

_____

_____

_____

_____

While some of the things listed may seem small, try doing without them for a couple of days and you will be reminded how incredibly blessed we really are. How ungrateful is it when we do not have something, to ignore the multitude of things we do have? If looking at all you have and how many prayers He has already answered for you does not build your trust in Him. I do not know what will.

Finally, let's address doubt:

"Now if any of you lacks wisdom, he should ask God, Who gives to all generously and without criticizing, and it will be given to him. But let him ask in faith without doubting. For the doubter is like the surging sea, driven and tossed by the wind. That person should not expect to receive anything from the Lord. An indecisive man is unstable in all his ways." James 1:5–8

If you are just saying rote words at night and calling it prayer, it's not going to do you any good. To be successful in prayer, you must remember that you are bringing a petition before the God of heaven and your Creator. You must believe with your whole heart that He is there, that He has the ability to fulfill your request, and that He loves you and wants to take care of you. Regardless of the answer, know that He will give you the strength to endure it.

Trust is a very difficult uphill climb. The trial to wait can either make or break your relationship with God and your trust in Him. I encourage you to take a step today toward Him. You cannot do this without Him. Let down your guard, let go of fear, and trust Him to make your path straight.

Chapter 4

Waiting in Prayer

The key to any healthy relationship is communication. God has already communicated with us through His Word. We communicate back to Him through prayer. There are three aspects of a healthy prayer life I would like to discuss: Frequency, Honesty, and Thanksgiving.

Frequency:

> "Then you will call upon Me and come and pray to Me, and I will hear you. You will seek Me and find Me, when you seek Me with all your heart." Jeremiah 29: 12–13

> "Keep on asking, and you will receive what you ask for. Keep on seeking, and you will find. Keep on knocking, and the door will be opened to you." Matthew 7:7

> "Which of you, if your son asks for bread, will give him a stone? Or if he asks for a fish, will give him a snake? If you, then, though you are evil, know how to give good gifts to your children, how much more will your Father in heaven give good gifts to those who ask Him!" Matthew 7:9–11

"Then Jesus told His disciples a parable to show them that they should always pray and not give up. He said, "In a certain town there was a judge who neither feared God nor cared what people thought. And there was a widow in that town who kept coming to him with the plea, 'Grant me justice against my adversary.' For some time he refused. But he finally said to himself, 'Even though I don't fear God or care what people think, yet because this widow keeps bothering me, I will see that she gets justice, so that she won't eventually come and attack me!' And the Lord said, 'Listen to what the unjust judge says. And will not God bring about justice for His chosen ones, who cry out to Him day and night? Will He keep putting them off?'" Luke 18:1–7

"Rejoice in hope, be patient in tribulation, be constant in prayer." Romans 12:12

"Be persistent in prayer, and keep alert as you pray, giving thanks to God." Colossians 4:2

While I do not know when you will receive an answer, there is one thing I can guarantee: you will receive an answer. I do not know if you will receive it after your second prayer or after your two millionth prayer, but you will receive an answer. The key is to keep asking.

Believe it or not, this is a difficult task. After a few years of silence, it is very tempting to give up. Why would I keep baring my soul to a God who doesn't seem to hear or care? The answer is rather beautiful: because it is a burden He has to help you carry. Whatever you are waiting for, it is an open, painful wound in your heart. There are so many moments when it is just too much to carry alone. So our wise and merciful God gives us the opportunity to lean on Him as often as we need to. Every time we bring our heart's petition before His throne, we release ourselves from the burden and leave it in the capable hands of the Creator of the Universe. The more you take advantage of this, the easier it will become to navigate the trial.

Honesty:

> "Though He slay me, yet will I trust Him. Even so, I will defend my own ways before Him." Job 13:15

> "Trust in Him at all times, O people; pour out your heart before Him; God is a refuge for us." Psalm 62:8

> "The Lord is close to all who call on Him, yes, to all who call on Him in truth." Psalm 145:18

> "Let us therefore come boldly unto the throne of grace that we may obtain mercy, and find grace to help in time of need." Hebrews 4:16

> "Casting all your anxieties on Him, because He cares for you." 1 Peter 5: 7

The depth and success of a relationship depends on the quality of communication. I want you to ask yourself, how much do you actually let God in? Do you pray to Him like you are addressing a monarch or reading from a script or do you pour out your heart to Him like He is your best and oldest friend? While God is the Utmost and Highest, He has invited us to come before Him and be honest about how we feel.

Like any relationship, there will be moments of joy where we cannot help but smile through a prayer as we express our gratitude. In contrast, there will be moments of intense weeping where we cry out to God from our knees and scream, "WHY?"

It's easy to put on a "good face" around our acquaintances and pretend like everything is just fantastic in our lives. The Lord does not expect that from us. He wants us to open up to Him and tell Him how we feel and how much we need Him. It is okay to say, "Lord, this is a hard moment. I feel like my heart is breaking in my chest and I can't seem to stop crying. My faith is struggling and I don't know what to do or how to handle this. I know you hear me and I need you so badly right now. Please help me!" David did. So many times in the Psalms, we can read David pouring out the depths of his soul to God. As you journey through the same wilderness of pain, take a note out of his playbook, and let God know where you really are and how much you need Him.

Thanksgiving:

> "The Lord is my strength and my shield; my heart trusts in Him, and I am helped; therefore, my heart exults, and with my song I shall thank Him." Psalm 28:7

> "Give thanks to the Lord for He is good, His love endures forever." Psalm 118:29

> "Do not be anxious about anything, but in everything by prayer and supplication with thanksgiving let your requests be made known to God. And the peace of God, which surpasses all understanding, will guard your hearts and your minds in Christ Jesus." Philippians 4:6–7

> "Give thanks in all circumstances; for this is the will of God in Christ Jesus for you." 1 Thessalonians 5:18

> "Every good and every perfect gift is from above, coming down from the Father of lights

with Whom there is no variation or shadow due
to change." James 1:17

Gratitude creates perspective. I have sought to be very honest
with the depth of pain that comes with waiting, however, I would be
remiss if I did not also include different strategies for surviving and
thriving while waiting. While your prayer should be frequent and
honest, do not forget to be thankful.

In the previous chapter, we discussed multiple things that we
have been blessed with and how much we have to be thankful for. If
you allow your prayers to only be prayers of petition, your communication with God becomes selfish. It also becomes so much easier
to focus on what you do not have and allow your heart to become
embittered towards God because you feel that He is withholding
from you what you desperately need.

We all have a friend that asks for something every time we see
them. Either they are low on funds, they were unwise with their time
and need help completing a project, or they are just needy. How
would you feel if they never said "Thank you"? Offended, upset, and
greatly desirous for them to give back whatever you gave them? And
you feel fully justified in this because they do not have basic manners
and are not grateful for the sacrifices we made to help them.

Let's bring it to us. Our God absolutely showers us with blessings. How do you think we make Him feel when we behave like a kid
that got a hundred presents for Christmas but spent all day crying in
their room because they didn't get the one they wanted? It should be
a very humbling thought to embrace that you have behaved that way.
So have I. We need to fix our mind-set.

One of my friends gave me a gratitude journal for this year. The
goal is to fill in at least one thing you are grateful for each day, and
then pray to God and thank Him for it. Some days are more difficult than others, but it has been one of the best practices I have ever
undertaken. The more you are thankful for what you do have, the
less time you have to dwell on what you don't.

Like I said previously, gratitude creates perspective. Be thankful to God, even in the midst of trial. There is always, always, always something to be thankful for!

In closing, as you mold and shape your prayer life, something amazing will happen. You will find that you are a stronger person, a better person, and the promise of the Scripture will be fulfilled: you will have peace.

Chapter 5

Waiting in Action

"Then He said to His disciples, 'The harvest is plentiful but the laborers are few; therefore pray earnestly to the Lord of the harvest to send out laborers into His harvest." Matthew 9:37–38

"And let us not grow weary of doing good, for in due season we will reap, if we do not give up. So then, as we have opportunity, let us do good to everyone, and especially to those who are of the household of faith." Galatians 6:9–10

"Not that I am speaking of being in need, for I have learned in whatever situation I am to be content. I know how to be brought low, and I know how to abound. In any and every circumstance, I have learned the secret of facing plenty and hunger, abundance and need. I can do all things through Him who strengthens me." Philippians 4:11–13

"Whatever you do, work at it with all your heart, as working for the Lord, and not unto men." Colossians 3:23

"Let no one despise you for your youth, but set the believers an example in speech, in conduct, in love, in faith, in purity." 1 Timothy 4:12

"Do your best to present yourself to God as one approved, a worker who has no need to be ashamed, rightly handling the word of truth." 2 Timothy 2:15

"In everything set them an example by doing what is good. In your teaching show integrity, seriousness, and soundness of speech that cannot be condemned, so that those who oppose you may be ashamed because they have nothing bad to say about us." Titus 2:7–8

"But encourage one another day after day, as long as it is still called 'Today', so that none of you will be hardened by the deceitfulness of sin." Hebrews 3:13

While you are waiting, you have been given a precious gift: Time. It may not be a gift you particularly want. However, it has amazing potential and purpose. I entreat you not to throw it back in God's face and try to force His hand to get what you want. Give Him a chance to help you grow.

Allow me to provide some suggestions for how to use this time:

Have Bible studies: No matter how badly you may feel like you have it, there is always someone who has it worse off than you. Reach out to them, and try to help them find their path to God. Encourage them and lift them up. You will be amazed at how much lighter your own burden feels.

Be active in your local congregation: Teach Bible classes, attend studies during the week, spend time with your brethren, reach out to people that you may not speak to very often, see if there are any extra opportunities to serve, and do what you can. Grow closer to your church family.

Pursue a goal: Go to school, take a trip, apply for your dream job, start a business…whatever you can dream up, do it!

Try new things: Move to a different place, write a book, paint a picture, learn how to play an instrument, form a new hobby, exercise, read more, eat healthier, learn a new language…again, if you can dream it, do it!

Visit friends and family: You may have friends or family that are in need of some help or just want your company. Use this time to bask in their love and presence.

Volunteer your time: Whether it's for a pet rescue, a hospital, food shelter, or people from church who need a smiling face, give them some of your moments.

Build your relationship with God: Discover who you really are and reflect on who you want to become. Read His word, do personal Bible study workbooks, communicate with Him, work on areas of weakness, shore up areas of strength, deal with old demons and past pains, allow Him to heal you and guide you, and let your love for Him and trust in Him grow.

Enjoy quiet time: Grab some coffee or tea, turn on some calming music, and just relax. Allow your brain to slow down a little bit and be at peace.

Spend time outside: Turn off and put down all of your screens and be in God's creation. Let its beauty surround you and fill you up with joy.

Have FUN!: Hang out with friends, go to the movies, eat at really good restaurants, go to concerts, go to theme parks, go to the beach, go to the zoo, go camping, take a road trip, host a game night, or whatever it is you like to do for fun. Don't allow pain to rule your life. Live it!

Time is a precious gift. Instead of trying to avoid it, look at it from a different angle and see the amazing possibilities. This trial will eventually pass. You do not want to look back on this season of your life with regret because you wasted the opportunity to grow from it. While you wait, use your time wisely, and you will be blessed for it.

What can you do this week with your time?

_____

_____

_____

_____

Chapter 6

Waiting in Humility

"Be still, and know that I am God. I will be exalted among the nations, I will be exalted in the earth!" Psalm 46:10

"He has told you, O man, what is good; and what does the Lord require of you but to do justice, and to love mercy, and to walk humbly with your God?" Micah 6:8

"Humble yourselves, therefore, under the mighty hand of God so that at the proper time He may exalt you." 1 Peter 5:6

I want to take a moment to dive a little deeper into the heart. I need you to please ask yourself a very serious question: have you allowed the trial of waiting to cause you to grow bitter and angry toward God? Do you feel like Satan has you on the rack and he is rolling the wheel and causing more and more pain, while God stands to the side, watching, and doing nothing to stop it? Are you angry that after years of faithful service He has, all of a sudden, stopped listening to your prayers when you need Him the most? I was. And if that describes you as well, this chapter is for you.

It is very difficult to admit when your faith is wavering or extinguishing, to yourself or to others. I do not plan on spending any time berating you because of what you feel. I find that to be counterproductive and hypocritical. Instead, I encourage you to simply accept what you feel and, together, let's deal with it.

Entitlement: One word that describes the mind-set of humanity. We feel that, simply because we exist, we are owed. We can see the detriment this mind-set has had on society but nothing is worse than to carry it before the throne of God. We feel because of all that we have done, God owes us a happy life with nothing bad ever happening to us. Allow me to address this with two points:

1.   God never promises that.

Have you ever heard someone justifying his or her sinful decisions by saying, "I know God wants me to be happy"? I can confidently say that God never says that.

What He does say is this:

> "Strengthening the souls of the disciples, encouraging them to continue in the faith, and saying that through many tribulations we must enter the kingdom of God." Acts 14:22

> "For I consider that the sufferings of this present time are not worth comparing with the glory that is to be revealed to us." Romans 8:18

> "No temptation has overtaken you that is not common to man. God is faithful, and He will not let you be tempted beyond your ability, but with the temptation He will also provide the way of escape, that you may be able to endure it." 1 Corinthians 10:13

> "Blessed is the man who remains steadfast under trial, for when he has stood the test he will receive the crown of life, which God has prom-

ised to those who love Him. Let no one say when he is tempted, 'I am being tempted by God', for God cannot be tempted with evil, and He, Himself tempts no one." James 1:12–13

"In this you rejoice, though now for a little while, if necessary, you have been grieved by various trials." 1 Peter 1:6

"And after you have suffered a little while, the God of all grace, who has called you to His eternal glory in Christ, will Himself restore, confirm, strengthen, and establish you." 1 Peter 5:10

2.   You are not as owed as you may think.

While you may be a faithful servant of God, you are not perfect. None of us should look at God as if we are owed. If we received what we deserved from God all of us would go to hell. Thankfully, God already paid the price for our lives and our souls.

"For God so loved the world, that He gave His only Son, that whoever believes in Him should not perish but have eternal life." John 3:16

"For all have sinned and fall short of the glory of God." Romans 3:23

"For while we were still weak, at the right time Christ died for the ungodly. For one will scarcely die for a righteous person—though perhaps for a good person one would dare to die—but God shows His love for us in that while we were still sinners, Christ died for us." Romans 5:6–8

"But thanks be to God, that you who were once slaves of sin have become obedient from the heart to the standard of teaching to which you were committed, and having been set free from sin, have become slaves of righteousness." Romans 6:17–18

"For the wages of sin is death, but the free gift of God is eternal life in Christ Jesus our Lord." Romans 6:23

"But each person is tempted when he is lured and enticed by his own desire. Then desire when it has conceived gives birth to sin, and sin when it is fully grown brings forth death." James 1:14–15

I do not bring these things to your attention to shame you; I simply want to help you shape your mind-set. Satan is filling your head with lies, and the only way out is to fill it with truth: God has never left you. He is listening to your prayers. He loves you so much. He has never promised you an easy, happy, simple life. He promised that there would be trials, but He also promised that He would help you through them. God does not owe you anything. He has already rescued you and blessed you. He is God, and He sees the big picture. He knows what you need before you ask. He will be with you every step of the way and will carry you when you cannot take any more steps.

The farther you allow yourself to get from God, the worse the trial will be and the more your heart will break. Satan has nothing to offer you except lies, guilt, pain, and death. He will do everything he can to break you and destroy you. Never underestimate how much he hates you. He wants you to leave God because then you are easier to take down. He wants you to suffer not only in this life but also for all eternity. Please don't allow him to fill your mind with lies any longer. Break the chains of anger and bitterness that he has put around your heart and give it back to God. That is the only way you will survive.

Take a deep breath. Now, start in the direction of humbling your heart before God. Let your attitude be one of trust. You will have moments where you falter, but let them be just that, moments. Know that He sees so much more than you could ever imagine. He is working and needs you to be right where you are so that He can accomplish amazing things in your life. He's got you, dear friend. He's got you. He may have to break you and mold you, but please know it is not without purpose. He is trying to take you to the next step. If He has to use the trial of waiting to accomplish that, so be it. Humble yourself under His hand and let Him shape your life into one of blessing and beauty.

Chapter 7

Waiting in Honesty

"Now when Job's three friends heard of all this evil that had come upon him, they came each from his own place, Eliphaz the Temanite, Bildad the Shuhite, and Zophar the Naamathite. They made an appointment together to come to show him sympathy and comfort him. And when they saw him from a distance, they did not recognize him. And they raised their voices and wept, and they tore their robes and sprinkled dust on their heads toward heaven. And they sat with him on the ground seven days and seven nights, and no one spoke a word to him, for they saw that his suffering was very great." Job 2:11–13

"A friend loves at all times, and a brother is born for adversity." Proverbs 17:17

"And though a man might prevail against one who is alone, two will withstand him—a three-fold cord is not quickly broken." Ecclesiastes 4:12

"Bear one another's burdens, and so fulfill the law of Christ." Galatians 6:2

One of the temptations of waiting is the desire to isolate yourself. It is very easy to look around you and see that the hole you have in your heart is filled in the lives of everyone who surrounds you. You see couple after couple, family after family, healthy individual after healthy individual…and you feel so alone. I would like to project that is exactly what Satan wants you to feel. He wants you to feel so left out and alone that you begin to believe that is what life holds for you and reject the promises of God. He wants to fill your heart with despair, depression, and fear. Since I take great joy in not giving him what he wants, I would like to remind you that you are not alone.

I would encourage you to be honest with your trusted friends and family members about your struggle. There may not be very many in your life that you trust enough to confide in, and that's okay. Allow me to point out that Job was a very famous and wealthy man, however, in his time of need, only four people came to his aid, but four people came. Solomon says that you just really need one to two other people in your corner to help you through the difficult times. If you cry out for help, those who love you will come. The key is you have to humble yourself and let them in.

Share with them the pain and struggle. Share your weak moments and fears. Share your desire to pass this test. Share your hopes and dreams. Share your victories. Let them in so that they can help you. Waiting is a daily battle and you will need help. The ones in your corner will love you whether you are single, childless, and sick, or married, with children, and healthy. They love you for you. Pray about it together and let them hold you together while you make this journey.

God has blessed you with a support system, use it. I would like you to write down at least three people that you feel comfortable letting in to the depths of your heart. Spend some time thanking God for putting them in your life.

When you are finished, schedule some time this week to sit down with them and have a heart to heart. Be honest with them about your struggles and let them lift you up in prayer to the Lord. No matter what you are waiting for, the Lord never intended for you to wait alone. Even if you think friends/family do not understand what you're going through—they don't have to—they just need to be there for you, to sit with you, hold you, cry with you, pray with you, talk with you, laugh with you, have fun with you, love you, protect you, guide you, and hold your heart in safety while you navigate this uncharted territory.

Chapter 8

Waiting in Love

"I also could speak as you do, if you were in my place; I could join words together against you and shake my head at you." Job 16:4

"A word fitly spoken is like apples of gold in a setting of silver." Proverbs 25:11

"For by your words you will be justified, and by your words you will be condemned." Matthew 12:37

"Rejoice with those who rejoice, weep with those who weep." Romans 12:15

"If possible, so far as it depends on you, live peaceably with all." Romans 12:18

"Love is patient and kind; love does not envy or boast; it is not arrogant or rude. It does not insist on its own way; it is not irritable or resentful; it does not rejoice at wrongdoing, but rejoices with the truth. Love bears all things, believes all things, hopes all things, endures all things. Love never ends." 1 Corinthians 13:4–8

"With all humility and gentleness, with patience, bearing with one another in love."
Ephesians 4:2

"Above all, keep loving one another earnestly, since love covers a multitude of sins."
1 Peter 4:8

I would like to set aside a little bit of time to talk to those of you who are waiting beside someone. Currently, in your life, there is nothing pressing that you are waiting for. However, someone you deeply love is undergoing the trial of waiting. It is a difficult position to be in, and I thank you so much for being there for them. If you will allow me, I would like to help you mold your words and attitude toward them so that you can be helpful and not cause any unintentional pain.

Words are one of the most powerful weapons that human beings possess. They can build up and give the hearer courage and strength. They can also tear down and cause the hearer to become discouraged and weak. It is the latter I wish to discuss.

There are three common situations of waiting I would like to bring to your attention and humbly request that you listen to the pleas of someone who has been on the other end of unkind remarks. I have felt their sting and have shed my fair share of tears. While the person you love may not be comfortable enough to ask for your discretion, I would like to bring the need for it to your attention. Please remember Job's friends; they did great when they did not say anything, however, once they started speaking they only made Job's situation more painful.

Waiting for a spouse:

I have learned the hard way that others have a timeline for my life. If I do not graduate high school, go to college, get engaged, get married, and have children on their schedule, either something is wrong with me, or I have done something wrong.

Please understand, if the one you love is waiting for a spouse, there are a lot of emotions that go with it. To list a few: pain, embarrassment, loneliness, longing, isolation, despair, self-doubt, anger, and rejection. The worst thing you can do is cut even deeper into their wound with your words. Before you speak, remember their pain and struggle. Asking them questions such as, "Are you ever going to get married?" or "Why aren't you dating?" are not helpful. Try phrases such as, "You are a special treasure. I am so thankful God placed you in my life," or "How can I pray for you today?" Please do not attempt to offer help in finding them a spouse unless they ask for it. Don't allow yourself to define them by whether or not they are married. Get to know them. Lift them up and find out how you can be of help to them in their growth as a Christian. You do not know what God has planned for their life. Work to help them achieve it and be patient with them while they strive to attain it.

Waiting to expand their family:

I would like to start this section with a story: A married couple has prayed about it and decided they would like to try to have a baby. The journey begins with excitement that slowly fades into anxiety and pain after the tests continue to come back negative. One Sunday morning, the wife takes her fiftieth pregnancy test and, again, it comes back negative. She breaks down on the floor of the bathroom in heaving sobs. Her heart is shattered to find out that her arms will remain empty. The husband hears her, comes in, and finding her crying on the floor, wraps her in his arms, and they cry together until there are no more tears left. After praying, they decide the only place to find comfort is in the house of God, and they manage to make their way to worship. They are a few minutes late and sit in the back. The entire service they are holding hands, praying, and finding some soothing for the deep ache in their hearts. They planned on making a quick exit after services, however, one older lady catches her before she can leave and asks, "You and your husband have been married long enough, when are you going to start a family?"

How do you think that made her feel? I wish I could tell you that I made up this story. Unfortunately, it is the story of so many women. I have held them as they cried to me. I hope it breaks your heart as it did mine and I hope that it brings you to think carefully about what you say.

I would like to make a few blanket statements that I understand may offend, but they need to be said. If a couple has been married for more than one day:

How they plan to expand their family, or if they plan to expand their family, is not your business. It does not matter if you are the mother, grandmother, mother-in-law, sister, aunt, father, father-in-law, brother, uncle, family friend, or random acquaintance. That is a decision between them and God. Their sex life is none of your business. If they want to tell you about their family planning, that is for them to bring up to you, not the other way around.

If they choose to adopt, that is a decision worthy of joy and praise, not negativity. There is nothing more beautiful or selfless than to adopt a precious child into your family.

There is no need to place unnecessary pressure by saying things like, "When are you going to give me grandchildren?" or "You don't want to wait too long before you start a family." Again, regardless of who you are, it is not your business.

Allow them to enjoy marriage. If they want to start a family and are having to wait, lift them up with prayer and encourage them. Help them grow as Christians. Pray for their marriage. If they let you in, encourage them to work on their marriage. Waiting for a child can be very taxing and difficult on marriages. Encourage them to continue to grow as a couple and with God while they wait.

Waiting for healing:

If your loved one has been diagnosed with a disease and is hoping and waiting to be cured, it is another long and difficult road. In many cases, I have been told that people just do not know what to say. Some helpful suggestions are, "You are always in my prayers" or "I appreciate the updates you give so that I can be more specific in my prayers." If you ask, "What can I do to help?" and they do not know, please don't be offended. They may not actually know. I will say that grocery store gift cards, food, and offers to help clean the house go a long way. I would encourage you not to give any medical advice unless asked. Trying to politely decline endless offers of advice is very taxing. Love them with patience. Please try to understand that in the midst of the trial of waiting, they are also trying to come to grips with the fact that the answer may be no. There is a lot of fear and anxiety that comes with that. Hold them when they cry. Take them back to the Lord who will help soothe their anxiety and calm their fears. Encourage them to stay faithful to the Lord, no matter what happens, because He will be with them and give them strength.

For those of you who are waiting, I would like to make a brief statement to you. I do understand the pain that words can bring. Believe me. However, in those moments, I would encourage you to hold your tongue, and try to maintain peace. Please remember, that, in their way, they may be genuinely trying to help you. They are trying to show you that they care and they love you. Or they are just trying to reach out to you and make small talk. Are they doing it wisely or well? No. But they are still trying. Lashing out at them will not be productive. I would advise you to absorb and deflect. Come up with a blanket answer like, "No, but I trust in the Lord and His timing. How are you? Tell me what is going on in your world." It will not get rid of the pain of their words, but your wisdom with your words will keep further pain from being caused. After your conversation is finished, Let. It. Go. That is the most important piece of advice I can give. If you do not it will well up inside of you, and you will begin to have bitterness in your heart toward the person who hurt you. Let it wash over you like water over a rock. I would also encourage you not to gossip to others about it and add sin to pain. Take the high road and maintain peace.

If both groups—the one who is waiting and the one who is beside them—are wise with their words, a lot of unnecessary pain can be avoided. Instead of allowing curiosity to cause you to hurt someone, try to get to know him or her as a person. Spend time with them and build a relationship as Christians. Help them grow closer to the Lord. Let them know that you love them, no matter what they have or do not have. If they let you in, go to the Word of God to help them endure. If they do not, pray for them to endure and to receive an answer. Either way, you are bearing their burden with them and helping them on their difficult path.

In closing, I would encourage us all to remember 1 Corinthians 13 and to love each other selflessly; be patient with each other even when you do not understand; be kind in your words and actions toward each other; do not envy the blessings another has; do not boast of the blessings you have; do not look down on another because they are without; do not be rude to each other; do not be easily set off; do not hold bitterness in your heart toward each other; do not rejoice in sin or gossip about it; rejoice with each other in the victories, blessings from God, and answered prayers; shelter each other from the storm of life; believe in each other; hope for the best for each other; hold each other up through thick and thin; and carry your love for each other to eternity.

Chapter 9

Waiting in Hope

"Behold, the eye of the Lord is on those who fear Him, on those who hope in His steadfast love." Psalm 33:18

"And now, O Lord, for what do I wait? My hope is in You." Psalm 39:7

"Why are you cast down, O my soul, and why are you in turmoil within me? Hope in God; for I shall again praise Him, my salvation and my God." Psalm 43:5

"But the Lord takes pleasure in those who fear Him, in those who hope in His steadfast love." Psalm 147:11

"Therefore the Lord longs to be gracious to you, and therefore He waits on high to have compassion on you for the Lord is a God of justice; how blessed are all those who long for Him." Isaiah 30:18

"And not only that, but we also rejoice in our afflictions, because we know that affliction produces endurance, endurance produces proven character, and proven character produces hope. This hope will not disappoint us, because God's love has been poured out in our hearts through the Holy Spirit who was given to us." Romans 5:4–5

"But if we hope for what we do not see, we wait for it with patience." Romans 8:25

"We have this hope as an anchor for the soul, firm and secure." Hebrews 6:19

"Let us hold fast the confession of our hope without wavering, for He who promised is faithful." Hebrews 10:23

"For you have need of endurance, so that when you have done the will of God, you may receive what was promised." Hebrews 10:36

"Now faith is the assurance of things hoped for, the conviction of things not seen." Hebrews 11:1

"Blessed be the God and Father of our Lord Jesus Christ! According to His great mercy, He has caused us to be born again to a living hope through the resurrection of Jesus Christ from the dead." 1 Peter 1:3

"Therefore, preparing your minds for action, and being sober-minded, set your hope fully on the grace that will be brought to you at the revelation of Jesus Christ." 1 Peter 1:13

"He will wipe away every tear from their eyes, and death shall be no more, neither shall there be mourning, nor crying, nor pain anymore, for the former things have passed away."
Revelation 21:4

Imagine you are standing in front of a huge white wall. Directly in the center of the wall is a pinpoint black dot. You walk toward the wall and, with a drinking straw in hand, place it over the dot and look inside. All you are going to see is black. Everything in your line of sight is shadowed and small. It doesn't matter if the rest of the wall is white; you are focused on the one small spot that is not.

My friends, that is so often what we tend to do with our lives. When we have a black dot of waiting on the canvas of our hearts, it can so easily become all we focus on. The more we focus on it, the more despair will set in until the situation seems hopeless. I would like to take some time to discuss with you the importance of keeping hope alive.

Hope changes everything. We can endure even the worst of circumstances if we know there is an end date and something better is waiting on the other side. I can safely promise you, there will be an end date. You will receive an answer, in God's perfect time. It will be okay! And there is something infinitely better on the other side; Not only will your relationship with God be stronger, but you will be a better person, and you will be one step closer to the actual goal of heaven!

That, dear friends, is the only thing that matters! No matter the circumstance or situation, it will be brightened with the hope of heaven. I love the line in the hymn, "Just one glimpse of Him in glory will the toils of life repay." Truer words have never been spoken. So when your moments are dark, step back and try to see the big picture.

Another interesting thing to consider, your trial of waiting may not actually be about you. As I have said before, there is a much bigger picture that only the Lord can see. The timing of your life has to be perfect because it affects so many other lives; not just of those around you but also from those who will come from you. Your season of waiting may be because your future spouse is not ready for you yet, your children must be born or brought into your family at the perfect time for their future to be timed just right, the cure is still in the process of being approved, someone you meet at treatment needs to hear the Gospel, or there will be a soul you will come in contact with in the future that is going through the same trial who needs your help. The possibilities are endless, and the timing must be perfect.

Even in the darkest and worst of circumstances, the Lord never asks us to go without hope. As the writer of Hebrews says, it is the anchor of the soul; the only thing that will help us weather the storm. Our anchor is provided from the Lord each and every day. The key is to step back from the wall and realize that it is full of white!

I am both a geek and a nerd, and I love *The Lord of the Rings*. Samwise makes a statement in the *Two Towers* that really hits home for me. When discussing with Frodo why they should go forward with this difficult, dangerous, and seemingly impossible task, he says, "Because there is some good in this world and it is worth fighting for." Applying that to us, there is so much hope for the Christian and it is worth holding on to and fighting for. Please do not give Satan your dreams and hopes for the future in exchange for despair. Don't give up the battle before it is even over. Do not resign yourself to a life of misery, the Lord has so much more planned for you!

While you wait, do not give up hope! Not only hope that your prayer will be answered but, most importantly, the hope that comes from God's promises. No matter how your situation turns out, in a very short time, it won't matter anymore because you will be safe in the embrace of the Lord and free from pain. You will have the ultimate prize. Let your heart be free to hope and let it light up even the darkest of nights.

As we draw this chapter to a close, I would like to provide a few tactics I have used to help keep hope alive. I have many moments, mostly at night when all is quiet, and I am alone, that I feel the bars of despair closing around my heart. I am probably not alone in that.

While I am far from perfect, here are some things I use to keep my heart calm and my eyes focused on the goal of heaven.

Immediately start praying.

I need the line of communication to God open as quickly as possible to withstand the temptation. While undergoing the trial of waiting, you are already in a weakened state. Make sure you have God in your corner.

Reach out to a trusted friend.

Look back at your previous list of loved ones. When you feel the despair start to settle in, contact them and let them talk you through it.

Allow yourself to cry.

God gave us this wonderful means to release emotions. Use it! There is absolutely no shame in releasing your grief, fear, anxiety, and anger in the form of tears.

Read through Scriptures and recite them over and over.

The reason I started this study with verses is because those are my main weapons to fend off attack. It helps you to refocus and gives you more positive words to fill your mind and heart.

Speak words of truth.

Whether it's "No matter what happens, God will give me strength to deal with it," or reciting and meditating on Philippians 4:8. Say it out loud so that you can drown out the lies of Satan.

Listen to Gospel music.

I cannot tell you how many times I have fallen asleep to the beautiful music and messages of hymns. The notes and words have such a soothing effect on my soul that I am finally able to relax and refocus.

Start doing something for someone else.

If Satan attacks you during the day, get busy. Fill your hands with something. Even if you make brownies for your neighbor, reach out to a friend in need, make dinner for someone, or help someone clean, do something that takes your mind off yourself and puts it on the needs of another.

Count your blessings.

There is nothing in this world that is so successful at creating gratitude and calming fears like focusing on how much God has already done for you. Get out a piece of paper, number it, and start listing your blessings until you feel the wave of anxiety ebbing.

Reflect on all that He has already accomplished in Your life.

If your trust in God is being attacked, look behind you and see the path He has already paved so carefully and lovingly for you to walk on. He was with you then and He has not left you now.

I encourage you to come up with a few of your own. The more prepared you are for Satan to attack your hope, the harder it will be for him to take it from you.

_____

_____

_____

_____

Fix your eyes steadfastly on the One who loves you the most and greatly desires to bless you. Keep hope firmly secured in the depths of your heart and know, with no doubting, He has got you and He will carry you all the way through life and into eternity. Follow Him by faith and trust His wisdom and timing. Heaven will surely be worth it all!

Chapter 10

Waiting for the Lord

"Indeed, none of those who wait for You will be ashamed; Those who deal treacherously without cause will be ashamed." Psalm 25:3

"Lead me in Your truth and teach me, for You are the God of my salvation; For You I wait all the day." Psalm 25:5

"Wait for the Lord; Be strong and let your heart take courage; Yes, wait for the Lord." Psalm 27:14

"Be strong, and let your heart take courage, all you who wait for the Lord." Psalm 31:24

"Our soul waits for the Lord; He is our help and our shield." Psalm 33:20

"Rest in the Lord and wait patiently for Him; Do not fret because of him who prospers in his way, because of the man who carries out wicked schemes." Psalm 37:7

"I waited patiently for the Lord; and He inclined to me and heard my cry." Psalm 40:1

"My soul, wait in silence for God only, for my hope is from Him." Psalm 62:5

"I wait for the Lord, my soul does wait, and in His word do I hope. My soul waits for the Lord more than the watchmen for the morning; indeed, more than the watchmen for the morning." Psalm 130:5–6

"O Lord, be gracious to us; we have waited for You, be their strength every morning, our salvation also in the time of distress." Isaiah 33:2

"Yet those who wait for the Lord will gain new strength; they will mount up with wings like eagles, they will run and not get tired, they will walk and not become weary." Isaiah 40:31

"The Lord is good to those who wait for Him, to the person who seeks Him. It is good that he waits silently for the salvation of the Lord." Lamentations 3:25–26

"But as for me, I will watch expectantly for the Lord; I will wait for the God of my salvation, my God will hear me." Micah 7:7

"But if we hope for what we do not see, with perseverance, we wait eagerly for it." Romans 8:25

The writers of Psalms combine waiting with courage. I am so thankful that they do this because it is so true! This is a very difficult trial and one that requires a lot of courage to endure. One of my favorite quotes about courage is "Courage is not the absence of fear but the understanding that something is more important than fear." In this case, what is more important is the timing of the Lord and His desire for me to know that the best and most wonderful blessings are from Him.

Before this season in your life, you were a caterpillar. Things were simpler and you had everything you needed: plenty of leaves to eat and camouflage to keep you safe. However, that was not how you were intended to stay. God had a bigger and better plan. Circumstances led you to form a cocoon of waiting. In this cocoon, the Lord is shaping and molding you. He is changing you into something completely different but more beautiful than you could ever imagine. I pray when you emerge from this season, you will be a beautiful butterfly. Your wings will be filled with glorious color and your senses will be awakened as you take flight to heights you did not even believe possible. It is my hope for you that you will look back on this season of difficulty and pain, see where it brought you and how the Lord was able to accomplish such amazing things in your life and say, "It was worth it."

My precious friend, this is simply a season of your life. I do not know how long it will last, but one day, it will merely be a dark memory in the mist. While you wait for your prayers to be answered, use the time to your advantage instead of letting it control you. Strive to see the blessings and the positives of this season, and thank God for them. Let Him form and shape your life in His perfect time. It will be worth the wait!

CPSIA information can be obtained
at www.ICGtesting.com
Printed in the USA
LVHW091041280820
664155LV00006B/959